WAKE UP

AND SMELL THE

TOLERANCE

A Journal to Forge a Better World

One Thought at a Time

RIYA AARINI

Disclaimer

The contents of this book are for informational purposes only. The author does not make any guarantees or promises as to the results that may be obtained from using this book, and you accept the risk that results will differ for each individual. To the maximum extent permitted by law, the author disclaims any and all liability in the event any information contained in this book proves to be inaccurate, incomplete, or unreliable, or results in any damage, injury, or loss. Any perceived slight of any group or individual is unintentional.

This publication is meant to be a valuable source of information for the reader but is not intended to be or constitute professional advice. Your use of the information in this book is at your own risk.

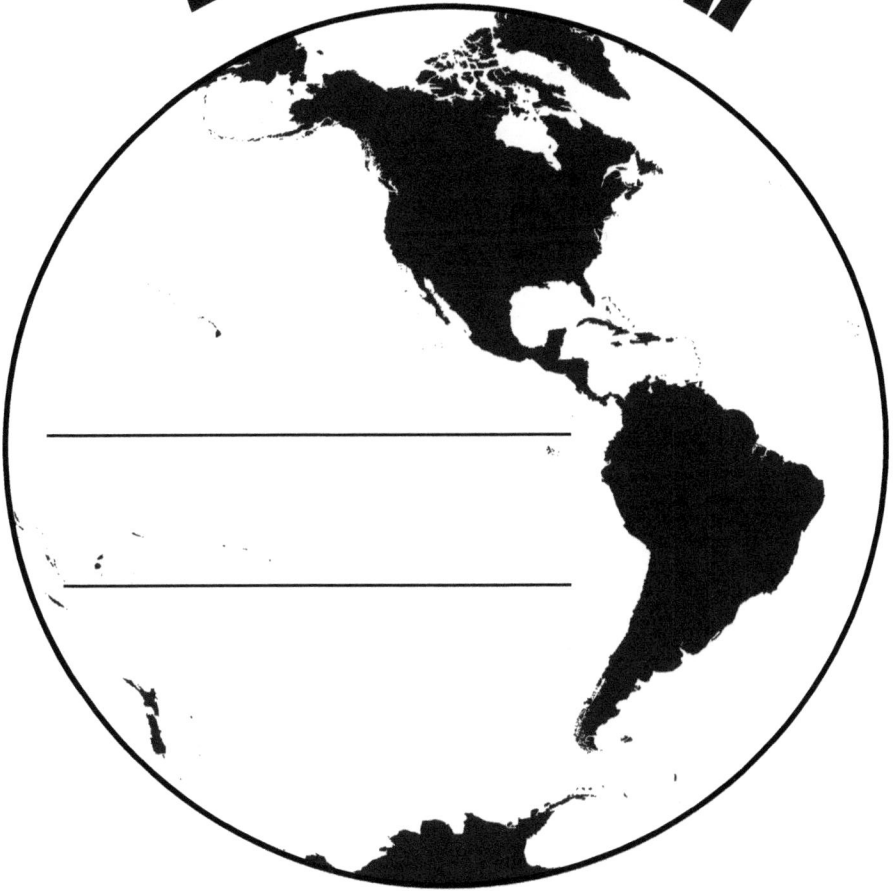

This journal

belongs to

Contents

Break the Illusion!

Intolerance is a universal ill, from Malayasia across the globe to Brazil. Failing to see beyond superficial differences makes accepting each other's humanity an ordeal. The United States, the world's most remarkable medley of ethnicities, is no less immune to its own brand of exclusivity.

Despite the pervasive hostility among humankind, it's possible to erase the bleakness, like the dawn surpasses the night. The illusion of inequality deludes much of humanity, but it can be overcome with a willingness to be open, a bit of effort, and a deep-dive into our subconscious minds.

Every person on Earth is ethnic—to someone else. A Japanese woman is ethnic to a Portuguese man. An Indonesian is exotic to a French Canadian. An American is ethnic to a farmer in Mozambique. On and on it goes, making the world fabulously rich with the beauty of cultural and ethnic diversity.

What if we as a collective people embraced this splendid diversity? After all, it exists in the animal kingdom, the marine world, and in all the flora and fauna on Earth! Perhaps you're

1

already on the transformative journey of creating a more inclusive society, and is the reason you're giving this book a try. Hopefully, your answers will lead you closer to who you aim to be.

The prompts on these pages take you on a no-frills journey of self-inspiration, allowing you to explore your deep-seated and not-so-deep-seated personal views on cultural harmony.

By forging a better world, you improve your life in the process. Imagine how free it'd feel to set yourself alight from the heavy burdens of bias, fear, hate, anger, and misunderstanding—and replace the self-torment with inner tranquility and societal peace.

Answer these prompts honestly, and you might begin to loosen the tangles that ensnare you in a cycle of unnecessary anguish.

A better world...a better life starts with you.

Rights of Humanity

All people shall have the right to freedom of opinion.

All people shall have the right to freedom of association.

All people shall have the rights to peace, health, and happiness.

All people shall have the right to good relationships.

All people shall have the right to safety.

All people shall have the right to prosper.

All people shall have the right to equal opportunity.

All people shall have the right to fair treatment.

All people shall have the right to enjoy life.

Birth

What is the town and country where you were born?

_____

_____

Describe the beauty of this part of the world. What makes your birthplace stand out?

Provide the day, month, and year of your birth on the 300,000-year human timeline.

_____

Looking back, describe the political climate surrounding the time of your birth. Do you recall society being apprehensive about or accepting of people with different ethnic backgrounds?

Family Tree

Humanity is more blended than at first glance. Humans have been mixing since neanderthals partied with homo sapiens at archaic get-togethers. People haven't stopped intermingling since, due to endless opportunities for migration, global trade, and social interactions in our small, highly connected world.

List members of your family tree on the next page. Go as far back as you wish (you may need another sheet of paper).

Some people who probe into their past discover they're related to kings and presidents, as well as paupers and scoundrels—from both familiar and exotic nations.

FAMILY NAME

As you reconnect with your lineage to understand your cultural identity, what emotions does it evoke? Fascination, sadness, gratitude?

How do you believe your ancestors' lives impacted yours?

Does knowing your relatives' hardships, sacrifices, and joys give you perspective on life?

Do you feel a sense of belonging as you unearth your ancestors' cultural histories?

Some people who feel strongly against other ethnicities unknowingly have those very ethnic backgrounds in their family tree.

You dig far back into your family tree and stumble upon ethnic ancestors, who are a part of your lineage due to secret adoptions, name changes, hidden identities, or travels from distant regions. How do you react, and why?

Ethnic Pride

Describe your ethnic background.

How do you feel about belonging to this ethnic group? Pride, satisfaction, self-esteem?

Do you feel an appreciation for your ethnic heritage?

Provide a fun fact about your cultural heritage.

Do you know your cultural history? If so, narrate an impactful event in your cultural timeline.

Name three cultural values you hold, such as respect for elders, individualism, hospitality...

_____

_____

_____

Do you believe other individuals have the same right to enjoy their cultural heritage, history, and values? Why or why not?

Family and Community

Family and Community

Do you believe other individuals have the same right to enjoy their cultural heritage, history, and values? Why or why not?

How did your parents feel about people of different cultures?

Did their influence shape your personal views?

Did your family discuss various cultures at home? If so, recount one conversation and how it impacted your beliefs.

Did you grow up in a community with members of a similar cultural background? If so, how did you feel knowing everyone around you was "the same"?

How did your youth experiences affect your acceptance or rejection of other cultures?

Have you attempted to challenge your ideologies, perhaps by traveling the world or exploring other neighborhoods and encountering various ethnic groups?

Did your journeys alter your worldview?

As you are exposed to more diverse people over time, do you feel yourself growing out of your early life beliefs? If so, what sparks the change? If not, what locks you in the past?

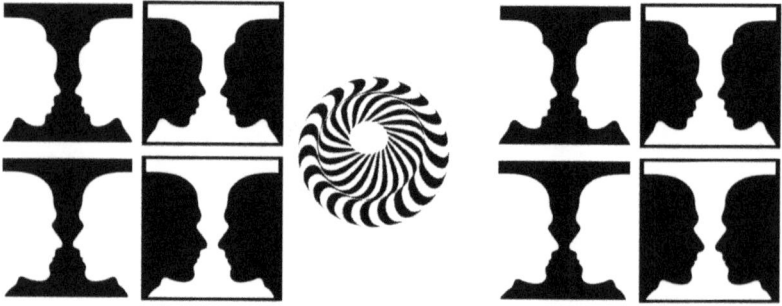

First
Introductions

Children often have little concept of "otherness" and engage in genuine fairness with peers, despite differences in skin tone, hair color, or other markers of ethnic identity.

What is your earliest childhood memory of a person of a different ethnicity? Someone you met, a television personality?

What was this person's name?

What do you believe was this person's ethnic identity?

How did you feel toward this individual?

What stirred these emotions?

As a child, did you engage with kids who belonged to different ethnic backgrounds? If not, why not?

If so, describe one memorable play event.

As you recollect, what emotions does the event inspire?

Can you bring this sense of innocence and openness to your interactions today? If not, what stops you?

Food

Do you enjoy ethnic food? If so, name an appetizing cuisine. Chinese, Mexican, Greek?

If not, why do you avoid eating dishes created by other cultures?

If you savor ethnic food, do you prefer it be adapted—or cooked authentically by the people from whose culture it originated? What influences your preferences?

Are you open to trying ethnic food, if given the opportunity? What conditions must be met, if any?

You are shipwrecked—stranded and starving on the shores of a desolate island. As you languish under the sun's scorching rays, a person from an exotic cultural background appears out of the blue, offering a cool drink and a plate of freshly cooked food.

Do you reject humanity and your own by refusing the life-saving gesture? If you accept the nourishing food and drink, what inclines you to do so?

As you satisfy your ravishing hunger, how do you feel toward this person?

Do differences in skin tone, hair color, or language matter at this point?

Do you share a conversation with this individual? What do you discuss?

If language is a barrier, is the universal language of kindness understandable?

Romantic Relationships

Are you involved in a romantic relationship?

If so, describe how much this person means to you.

List three endearing qualities in your partner.

_____

_____

_____

Your significant other metamorphoses into a person of a different ethnicity before your eyes. Yet they continue to share your core beliefs and interests. Do you still feel the same way toward them? Why or why not?

Do their jokes still make you laugh? Do their quirks still win you over?

If your partner and you chose each other, do you believe others have the same right to choose with whom they spend their life?

What emotions well up inside you when you see an interracial couple? Anger, rejection, betrayal? Warmth, consideration?

What are the thoughts behind these feelings?

Though love is universally felt, the experience is highly personal. What does romantic love mean to you?

How does the love between an interracial couple differ, if at all, from the love between your partner and you?

Does social evolution unhinge you? In other words, do you dislike change? If so, what do you fear?

When you notice interracial couples, what do you focus on? Their skin tone or their mutual love? Why?

Do you feel interracial couples are already challenged by cultural differences? Do you feel it's helpful to contribute to those difficulties?

Do you feel it's acceptable for romantic partners to have different hair and eye colors? If so, what makes different skin colors the game changer?

Struggles

Has the biting cold ever stung you, leaving you shivering and your teeth chattering?

How did the chill affect you?

Did you warm up? How incredible did the warmth feel?

If an impoverished man with an ethnic background similar to yours stole an electric blanket to keep his family warm in the depths of winter, would you justify it? Why or why not?

If a poor man from a different cultural background stole a USB cord to run a heater and keep his family warm under subfreezing temps, would you excuse it? Why or why not?

Describe the differences between these two people who committed petty crimes.

Describe the similarities between these two individuals who broke the law.

Goodwill

One stormy night, you pay for a meal for the car behind you in the fast-food drive-thru. You don't see who's driving, as the windows are tinted. Minutes later, your car stalls. The driver whom you'd treated pulls up with a jump. He steps out into the pouring rain, and you see he belongs to a different ethnicity.

As the rain beats down, do you pay attention to the good Samaritan's skin tone and language—or the jump in his hand?

You're on dialysis, miserable with kidney disease. Your doctor suggests a kidney transplant to improve your quality of life. You agree and are scheduled. After a successful surgery, you return to daily activities with newfound vigor. You wish to thank the donor. The transplant coordinator connects you with the living donor—who speaks with a non-native accent.

What do you say as you hold the phone, knowing this person's altruism gave you a new lease on life?

Have you ever had a long day? Describe how the exhaustion felt. A physical heaviness, a sense of time dragging?

The train is packed, and all the seats are taken. At the next stop, a tired-looking woman dressed in ethnic garb plods in with a toddler. You have the chance to provide relief.

Do you give up your seat? What motivates your action or inaction?

Do weariness—and relief—transcend cultural differences?

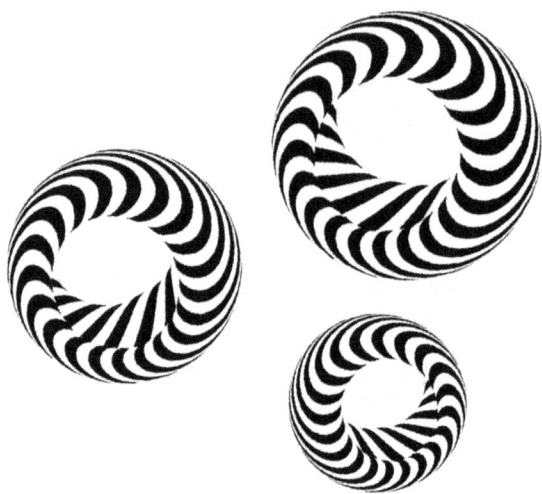

Furry Friends

Do you own a pet, such as a furry feline or canine?

Do you cherish the animal? What makes them so lovable?

You wake up one morning to find you've transformed into a seventy-pound chocolate labrador retriever. As you shake and stretch, puppies scramble into the room—your puppies, and they're all different colors: golden, chocolate, and black.

As the pups snuggle next to you, do you love them equally? Or do you favor some and reject others?

Does their fur color or personality determine your affection?

Does a person's skin tone or personality sway your feelings?

If your physical traits alone influenced others' sentiments, how would you feel, and why?

Us vs. Us

Outer differences manifest clearly yet camouflage the sameness underneath—the potential for feeling human emotions, like empathy and anger, and the need for life essentials, like social connection.

What does skin tone represent to you?

What does language represent to you?

What do cultural customs represent to you?

List five things you want out of life.

_____

_____

_____

_____

_____

Do you believe people with different skin tones, languages, or customs want the same life joys as you do? Love, respect, success, happiness, peace, comfort?

Or do you think they want things different than you? If so, like what?

Power

You win the lottery and are thrust into a position of enormous financial power. After buying mansions, cars, and a tropical island, you're still swimming in riches. You decide to help someone and come across a crowdfunding site. A brilliant, but poor, young woman hopes to start a research project to cure cancer. You consider donating a life-changing sum— pocket money to you—until you see her exotic name.

Do you donate or move on to another fundraiser? If you donate, what inspires your goodwill? If you continue scrolling, what motivates you?

Do you feel that supporting a person of a different cultural background undermines the progress of people of your cultural background? Or do you feel helping one well-intentioned person lifts all of humanity?

Limited
Resources

One of the principle drivers of hostility toward different ethnicities is rivalry amid scarce resources. Shelter, land, food, water, wealth, and even a sense of belonging are limited—yet crucial for survival.

Fierce competition pits people against each other as they attempt to increase their chances of providing for themselves. Differences in skin tone, language, or customs make ousting fellow humans seem easier.

How does the idea of infinite resources shape your views?

Land, from hills to valleys, and homes are in boundless supply. With plenty of land and housing for everyone, do you welcome neighbors of different ethnic backgrounds?

No matter where you set foot, fresh water and food are unlimited, continually replenishing and abundant. With no one vying for basic resources, do you feel accepting toward people of various cultural backgrounds? Why or why not?

You work your dream job in a location you prefer and earn triple your desired salary. These privileges are given to all alike. Without having to compete for jobs or pay, how open do you feel toward people with different skin tones? Why do you believe this is so?

The travel bug bites. You journey from the top of the world to the bottom, being invited to meals and celebrations by every ethnic group on the planet. Does their hospitality inspire a sense of belonging or increase your comfort with different cultures? If so, why?

Heroes

Who is your hero?

What qualities inspire your admiration of this person?

Unbeknownst to you, your hero possesses shapeshifting powers. One day they reveal their true identity as someone of exotic origins. Despite the revelation, they continue to express the qualities you admire.

Do you still consider this individual your hero? Why or why not?

Adverse Experiences

Did you ever have a terrible experience with someone from a different ethnic background? If so, describe the interaction.

What emotions did the event trigger?

Does this bad experience color your view of all ethnic people? If so, do you believe this is a fair judgment, considering you likely haven't met all the ethnic people in the world?

Do you feel this offender should be banished to a distant exoplanet? Or are they deserving of forgiveness?

If you choose forgiveness, what about them makes them human? Or if you prefer planetary exile, what bars you from forgiving them?

Describe a wonderful interaction you had with a person from a different culture.

Who was this person? What was their name?

Does this good experience influence your view of all ethnic people? If so, do you believe this is a reasonable assumption?

Did you ever have an awful experience with a person of a similar ethnic background as you? Narrate what happened.

What emotions ran through you?

Does this horrible experience shape your opinion of all people with the same ethnic background as you? If so, is this realistic?

Do you feel the offender should be launched into orbit and left to their own devices? Or do they deserve compassion? Why?

Did you ever have a good experience with a person of a similar cultural background as you? If so, recount the event.

What emotions did it stir up?

Does this positive interaction influence your opinion of all people who are culturally similar to you? If so, could this be an overestimation?

Have you ever intentionally offended a person of another culture? If so, describe the offense.

What was this person's name?

How do you think this person felt?

Do you believe you deserve their forgiveness? Why or why not?

Has a person with a different cultural origin forgiven you for a transgression? If so, what was the transgression?

Name the person who forgave.

How did you feel upon being forgiven?

Comedians

Humor exposes the worst of humanity—in the most harmless way. Stand-up comedians use this tactic and earn rounds of enthusiastic applause. Jokes are funny because at their core are fundamental truths we recognize.

Your friend takes you to a comedy club for a night of fun. A comedian with an ethnic background opens the show. He makes a string of ethnic jokes about stereotypes as well as differences and similarities between cultural groups—and you cannot help but to burst out in laughter.

As your hearty laughs release endorphins, the feel-good hormone, as well as oxytocin, which is linked with social bonding, do you feel a cathartic release? Perhaps a momentary freedom from intolerance?

What fills that gap? Trust, feelings of community, social connection?

Do you feel his ethnic humor further separates you from other cultures or draws you closer?

Do you appreciate this comedian, even briefly, for fostering good feelings?

Does your outlook on humanity change after the show? If so, what do you attribute this to?

Homogeneity

Do you like music? If so, name your favorite genre.

This genre is the only one that plays, in elevators, restaurants, offices. Do you grow bored without a repertoire of other music to add to your listening enjoyment?

Similarly, if all the music around you played a single note, could you enjoy a symphony or a rock song?

You live in a fanciful world populated by people with one skin tone. How do you feel? Safer, bored out of your mind, itching for variety?

If you believe you'd feel safer, would living in a homogenous society guarantee your safety? Why or why not?

Do people of different cultures add interest to the world around you? If so, how? If not, explain.

Stereotypes

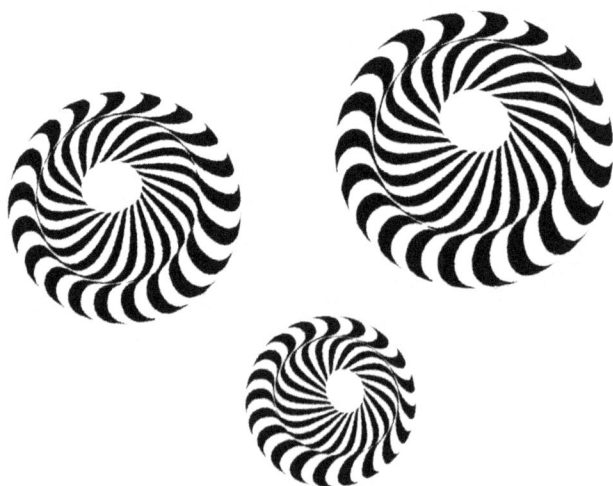

Stereotypes diminish unique characteristics, leading to misunderstandings, at best, and unjust treatment, at worst. Those who stereotype fail to see individual qualities and instead lump people together, mistakenly assuming they share the same attributes.

"All gnomes are good at physical labor" and "all mermaids win spelling bees" are examples of stereotypes. "Some gnomes excel at gardening, while others win spelling championships" is a non-stereotypical belief.

Do you subscribe to stereotypical beliefs, whether positive or negative? If so, provide an example of one you hold.

How does this stereotype help you make sense of the world and navigate society, if at all?

Or does holding the stereotype prevent you from seeing someone's genuine qualities?

For example, do you think all fairy-tale princesses are freeloaders, enjoying luxuries without paying for them? If so, have you ever known a selfless princess who gives to charity?

Does her generosity defy the stereotypical notion that all princesses are cheapskates?

Similarly, do you believe all elves are crooks? If so, do you think such stereotypes unfairly discredit the entire elf population?

Are you aware of any law-abiding elves? If so, does this test your assumption that all elves are alike?

Career

Do you work? If so, what do you do for a living?

Does your job give you the opportunity to meet people of different cultural backgrounds?

Do you feel it is a privilege to be exposed to global diversity at work?

Is it a challenge to work with people with diverse cultural backgrounds? If so, what do you attribute this to? Language, personality, work ethic?

Conversely, is it difficult to work with people of the same ethnicity as you? Why or why not?

Describe how, at the end of the day, all your colleagues work to achieve the same vision.

Do you feel your ethnic coworkers are driven by the same ambitions as you? If not, what do you believe sets you apart?

Have you ever received a promotion? If so, what was the basis of the promotion? Hard work, commitment, achievement?

Do you feel you deserved this promotion?

Has an ethnic colleague ever received a promotion? If so, how did they earn the promotion? Effort, resourcefulness, accomplishment?

Do you feel your colleague deserved this promotion?

If exceptional pay and career opportunities were awarded to everyone equally, would you feel secure when ethnic colleagues excelled? Why do you think so or not?

It's your birthday! Your family, friends, and colleagues have forgotten—except for that one coworker, who happens to be of ethnic origin. As you sit slumped in your chair, she stops by with a smile, a birthday wish, and a box of donuts she picked up at the bakery during her morning commute.

What do you say?

What emotions do you feel toward this colleague?

If, after her well-wishes, she receives a promotion, do you feel it's well-deserved?

Do you celebrate with her, perhaps with a box of donuts?

Interdependence

The coffee breaks you look forward to have strong Swedish influence. Similarly, many everyday items people enjoy have roots in diverse cultures. Smartphone components are mined in places, like South America; a single phone contains parts from dozens of countries.

Do you enjoy coffee? If so, does your coffee taste any less delicious when you learn their beans are planted, grown, and harvested by farmers in tropical parts of the world?

Does knowing the origins of commonplace goods or habits foster your appreciation for other people of the world?

Nations are suddenly closed off to each other, preventing the global exchange of goods and practices you highly value, whether that's chocolate, leaving shoes at the door, or something else. How do you respond?

Do you feel your identity grows stronger or weaker as a result of diverse cultural influences? Why?

Do you feel your world expand upon adopting customs of other countries?

Kindness

Has a person with a different ethnic background ever said nice words to you or done something kind for you? If so, describe the kind gesture.

What was this person's name?

What was their cultural background, if you could guess?

How did you feel upon receiving their kindness? Surprise, defiance, something else?

You cut a beached sea turtle from a fishing net. The turtle doesn't care what color your skin is or what language you speak; as it scurries away, all it appreciates is your kindness. A bystander of ethnic origin commends you for saving the marine animal.

How do you respond?

Do you accept his praise? Why or why not?

Is there a difference between the reactions from the sea turtle and the bystander—neither of whom judge you by your skin color but instead by your humanity?

Esteem

Has anyone ever complimented your amazing qualities? If so, share a memorable compliment you received.

Do you believe it? In other words, do you believe you possess this admirable characteristic?

You are the guest of honor at a surprise *tolerance party*. Guests of various ethnic backgrounds attend, bringing your favorite foods and gifting you desirable presents. They show they value you by roasting you—not with insults—but with compliments.

How do you react to being the center of adoration during this compliment roast and showered with goodwill from, what is to you, the unlikeliest sources?

Freedom

Do you still feel stuck in a cycle of anger fueled by bias?

How do you believe you'd feel if you released the intolerance—and invited inclusivity? Freedom, vulnerability, something else?

If you answered vulnerability, what would give you a feeling of security?

Do you believe you deserve to feel free? Why or why not?

Rights of Humanity

All people shall have the right to freedom of opinion.

All people shall have the rights to peace, health, and happiness.

All people shall have the right to good relationships.

All people shall have the right to safety.

All people shall have the right to prosper.

All people shall have the right to equal opportunity.

All people shall have the right to fair treatment.

All people shall have the right to freedom of association.

All people shall have the right to enjoy life.

As you near the completion of this journal, how do you now feel about these Rights of Humanity, which first appeared in the front of this book?

Do you notice a liberating shift in your ideologies? If so, describe how this change affects you. If not, write your own Rights of Humanity on the next page—rights you believe all human beings deserve equally.

Rights of Humanity

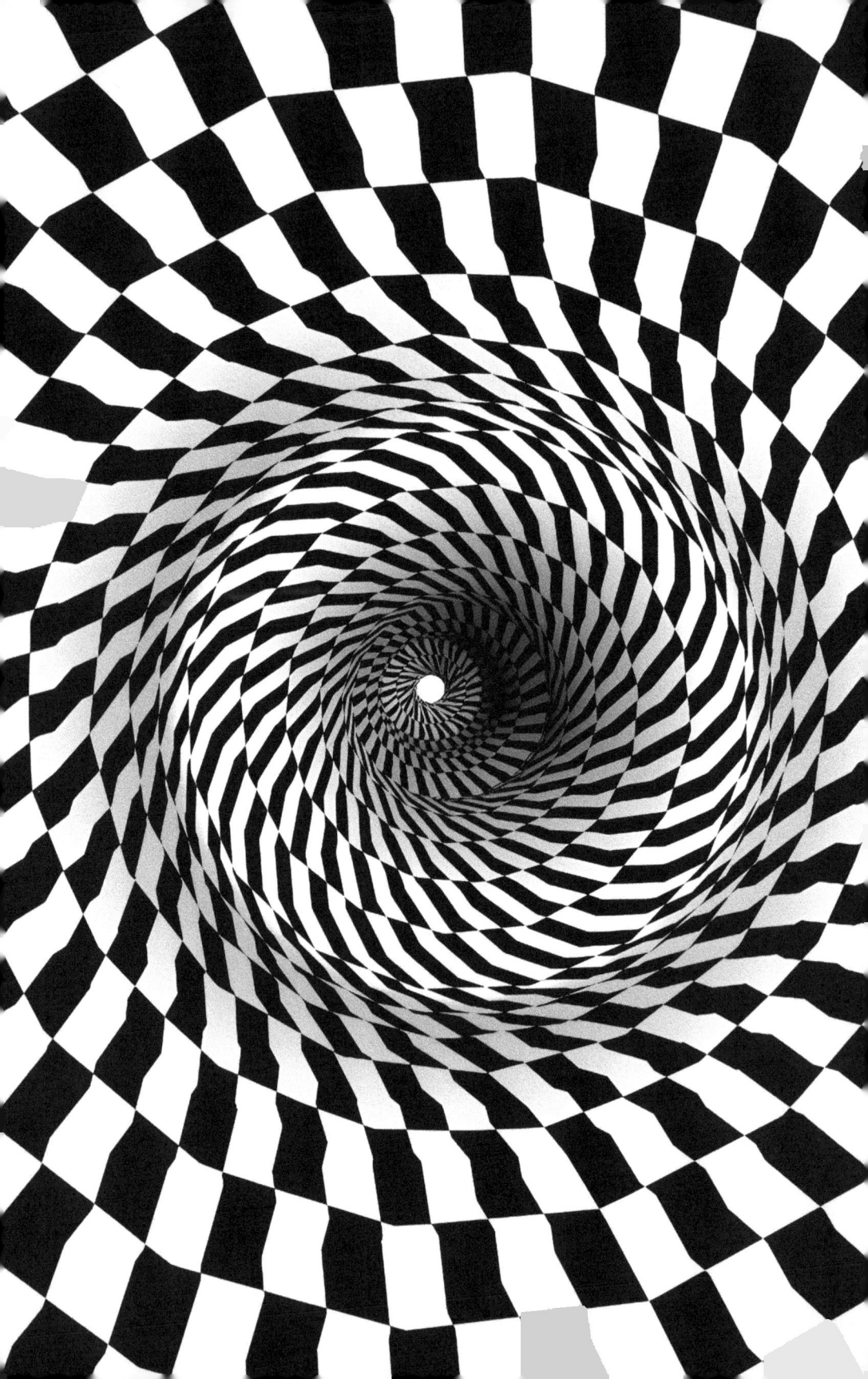

Out of the Abyss!

Cultivating an inclusive mindset is not only a personal victory but a triumph for humankind. It frees individuals and societies from the cold, unforgiving abyss of intolerance.

By exploring your beliefs in this journal, you've hopefully gained greater insights into how and why you feel the ways you do. Perhaps your answers inspire you to make amends with yourself and even others.

As humans, not one of us is perfect. But it's essential to remember we are all human.

Suksma

ngiyabonga

hvala ti

Děkuju

si Yu'os ma'ase

gràcies

Danke

Thank You!

Thank you for reading *Wake Up and Smell the Tolerance:*
A Journal to Forge a Better World One Thought at a Time.

If you found your time well spent, please consider sharing
your thoughts in a retailer review, and give others a path to
do the same. Your review is much appreciated!

Bedankt

Mahalo

obrigado

tak

dankon

Grazie

salamat po

merci

www.ingramcontent.com/pod-product-compliance
Lightning Source LLC
Chambersburg PA
CBHW052114030426
42335CB00025B/2982